A Note to Paren

D1646259

DK READERS is a compelling reading programme for children, designed in conjunction with leading literacy experts, including Cliff Moon M.Ed, Honorary Fellow of the University of Reading. Cliff Moon has spent many years as a teacher and teacher educator specializing in reading, and has written more than 140 books for children and teachers. He reviews regularly for teachers' journals.

Beautiful illustrations and superb full-colour photographs combine with engaging, easy-to-read stories to offer a fresh approach to each subject in the series. Each DK READER is guaranteed to capture a child's interest while developing his or her reading skills, general knowledge, and love of reading.

The four levels of DK READERS are aimed at different reading abilities, enabling you to choose the books that are right for your child:

Level 1 – Beginning to read
Level 2 – Beginning to read alone
Level 3 – Reading alone
Level 4 – Proficient readers

The "normal" age at which a child begins to read can be anywhere from three to eight years old, so these levels are only a general guideline.

No matter which level you select, you can be sure that you are helping your child learn to read, then read to learn!

LONDON, NEW YORK, MUNICH, PARIS,
MELBOURNE, AND DELHI

Project Editors Anna Lofthouse
and Caryn Jenner
Series Editor Deborah Lock
Senior Art Editor Cheryl Telfer
Project Art Editor Jacqueline Gooden
Art Editor Nicky Liddiard
DTP Designer Almudena Diaz
Production Shivani Pandey
Jacket Designer Chris Drew
Indexer Lynn Bresler

Reading Consultant
Cliff Moon, M.Ed.

Published in Great Britain by
Dorling Kindersley Limited,
80, The Strand, London WC2R 0RL

2 4 6 8 10 9 7 5 3 1

Copyright © 2003 Dorling Kindersley Limited, London

All rights reserved. No part of this publication
may be reproduced, stored in a retrieval system,
or transmitted in any form or by any means,
electronic, mechanical, photocopying, recording,
or otherwise, without the prior written
permission of the copyright owner.

A CIP catalogue record for this book is
available from the British Library.

ISBN 0-7513-4622-5

Colour reproduction by Colourscan, Singapore
Printed and bound in China by L Rex Printing Co., Ltd.

The publisher would like to thank the following for
their kind permission to reproduce their images:
c=centre, a=above, b=below, l=left, r=right.
2: Corbis: tr, br; 3: Corbis; 4: Getty Images/Image Bank bl;
5: ImageState tl, tr, cl, b; 6-7: Still Pictures; 11: Corbis t; 12: Corbis br;
13: Getty Images/Telegraph; 14-15: James Davis Travel Photography;
15: Corbis tr, Hutchison Library/John Hatt bc; 16: Corbis; 17: Corbis;
18: Corbis; 19: Getty Images/Image Bank br; 20: Getty Images/Stone;
21: Getty Images/Stone; 22: Corbis bl. 22-23: Powerstock Photolibrary;
24-5: Corbis; 25: ImageState c, Zefa tr; 26-7: Katz/FSP; 27: Agence
France Presse tr; 28: Apex Photo Agency/Simon Burt tl; 28-29:
alamy.com b, Zefa Picture Library t; 29: Apex Photo Agency/Simon cl;
30-31: NASA t; 32: Corbis tl, tr, cl, cr; 33: Corbis
All other images © Dorling Kindersley.
For further information see: www.dkimages.com

see our complete
catalogue at
www.dk.com

DK READERS

BEGINNING TO READ ALONE **2**

B48 108 057 0   MSC

SCHOOLS LIBRARY SERVICE
MALTBY LIBRARY HEADQUARTERS
HIGH STREET
MALTBY
ROTHERHAM
S66 8LD

SEP 2003

g

gs

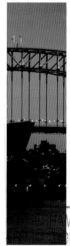

ROTHERHAM LIBRARY & INFORMATION SERVICES

This book must be returned by the date specified at the time of issue
as the DATE DUE FOR RETURN.
The loan may be extended (personally, by post or telephone) for a
further period if the book is not required by another reader, by quoting
the above number / author / title.

LIS7a

M LIBRARY &
N SERVICES

J720

B48 108 057 0

L /05190

SCHOOLS STOCK

A Dorling Kindersley Book

Think of a building –
an amazing building.
Does your building stand up tall?
Or does it spread out **wide?**
Is your building new,
with lots of shiny windows,
or is it old and made of stone?
Do you know how
buildings are made?

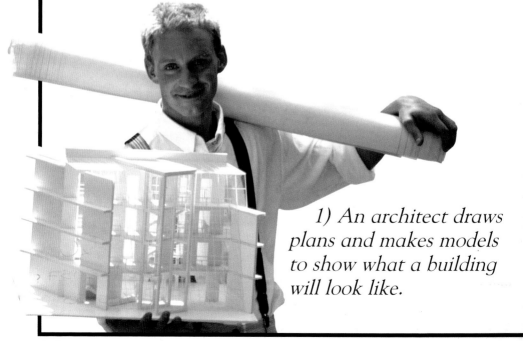

1) An architect draws plans and makes models to show what a building will look like.

2) The builders lay
strong foundations
in the ground.

3) They build the walls,
leaving gaps for the
windows and doors.

4) The sloping roof is
added and then glass
is put in the windows.

A big city like this has
all kinds of buildings –
tall buildings, wide buildings,
office buildings, factories and more.

There are weird and wonderful
buildings all over the world.
They are built to be useful,
as well as fun to look at.

The pyramids in Egypt
were built over 4,000 years ago.
These buildings were made
as burial sites for
Egyptian kings and
their treasure.

To build the pyramids,
workers had to drag heavy stones
up a ramp, one by one.

Many builders
It took 4,000 men
twenty years
to build the
biggest pyramid.

The pyramids were built
to last for many years.

The Ancient Romans
built a massive stadium
called the Colosseum.
The Romans were the first people
to use concrete
to make buildings.

The Colosseum was oval-shaped and seated up to 50,000 people. The Romans loved to watch trained gladiators fight each other. Cheers and boos from the crowd made echoes all around the stadium.

This fairy-tale castle, perched on a
craggy hilltop in Germany, is called
Neuschwanstein (NOY-shvan-stine).
Earlier castles were built
to protect the people inside,
who could spy on approaching
enemies from the tall towers.
But Neuschwanstein
was built just
to look pretty.

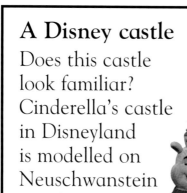

A Disney castle
Does this castle
look familiar?
Cinderella's castle
in Disneyland
is modelled on
Neuschwanstein
Castle.

One of the world's biggest palaces
is at Versailles (ver-SY) in France.
It has over 2,000 windows,
1,200 fireplaces and 67 staircases.
There is also a Hall of Mirrors
at Versailles.

When the palace
was built 300 years ago,
mirrors were very rare.
Visitors were amazed
to see their reflections.

Fit for a King
The King's bedroom
was at the centre
of the palace.
Louis XIV even
signed papers in bed!

The Eiffel Tower in Paris, France, is made of iron.

It was the tallest building in the world when it was built in 1889 and everyone was amazed to see it. In those days it was unusual to make buildings out of metal. Since then, metal has been used to make buildings taller and **taller.**

Extra strength

The criss-cross pattern of the metal bars gives the Eiffel Tower extra strength.

The tallest buildings of all
are called skyscrapers because
they seem to touch the sky.
The two Petronas Towers in
Malaysia are the tallest skyscrapers
in the world at 452 metres (1,483 ft).
Each tower has 88 floors.
Visitors can walk
from one building
to the other on
the Skybridge.

It takes a whole
month to clean
all the windows
on one tower!

Some buildings have big,
round roofs called domes.
The dome on Florence Cathedral
in Italy was difficult to build.
Builders made another dome
inside the cathedral to support
the huge outer dome.
Workers walked through passages
between the inner and outer domes.

The domes on
St. Basil's Cathedral
in Russia are called
onion domes.

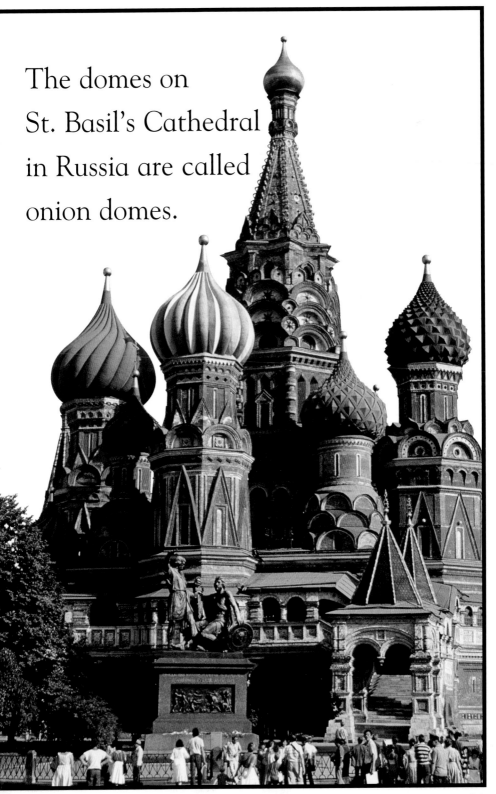

Have you ever seen a building
in the shape of a ball?
The round building in this picture
is called Spaceship Earth.
It is at the Epcot Centre
theme park in Florida, USA.
Over 11,000 triangles cover
the surface to make it look
perfectly round and white –
like a huge
golf ball!

More curves

This hotel in Dubai was designed to look like a wave at sea. It has 600 rooms for guests — all with sea views!

Think of the amazing shapes
of other modern buildings.
Can you guess what these buildings
are meant to look like?

The Sydney Opera House
in Australia looks like
the billowing sails
of a yacht.

The Guggenheim Museum in Spain may remind you of a large ship.

A gleaming roof
The roof of the Sydney Opera House is covered with over one million ceramic tiles.

Look at this huge building.
Stadium Australia was built for
the 2000 Olympic Games.
It was designed to be friendly
to the environment.
This means it uses less electricity
for lights and air conditioning.

Olympics
New stadiums are often built for special events, such as the Olympic Games.

The stadium has big tanks to collect rainwater that falls on the roof.
The rainwater is recycled to water the pitch and even to flush the toilets!

Where can you grow bananas indoors?
In a giant greenhouse!

At the Eden Project in England, the latest technology is used to create habitats from around the world.

Even when it's cold and dry outside, the weather is hot and damp inside the Humid Tropics Biome.

Jungle plants grow as if they are in the middle of a rainforest.

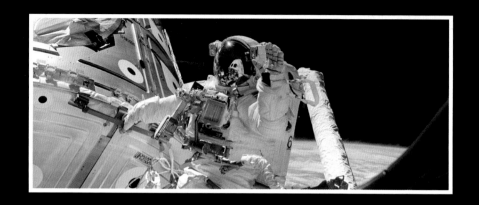

One of the most
amazing modern
buildings is way
out in space.

Every part of the International Space
Station comes from Earth
on board a space shuttle.
Who knows what other
amazing buildings may
be built in the future?

More building facts

A wide moat surrounds many castles, such as Raglan Castle in Wales. A moat is a ditch filled with water to keep enemies out.

The Ice Hotel in Canada is rebuilt every winter using fresh ice and snow. Every year, it looks different.

The Tower of Pisa in Italy sank into the soft soil on one side, causing it to lean. To prevent it falling down, scientists have given it special supports.

The Great Wall of China was built to keep out invaders. It is so long that it can be seen from space.

The World Trade Centre was a group of seven office buildings opened in New York City, USA, in 1973. Two of these buildings were 110-storey skyscrapers known as the twin towers – the tallest sights on the New York City skyline. On September 11, 2001, the twin towers and other buildings were destroyed in a terrorist attack.